PRIMER LEVEL

piano
student

By David Carr Glover
and Louise Garrow

David Carr Glover
PIANO LIBRARY

D1531606

The Piano Student - Primer Level
by
David Carr Glover and Louise Garrow

Foreword

The purpose of this piano primer is to present to the young piano beginner a concise, step by step approach to the study of the piano in either private or class lesson.

The materials are fresh and new and presented to insure steady progress toward a musical goal.

Supplementary materials should be used to balance the study material. Additional piano studies will promote good music reading and develop piano technic. For more primer solos and a complete thematic listing of all Glover/Belwin-Mills Publications, refer to the "Teacher's Guide for David Carr Glover Piano Library.

Materials Correlated with "The Piano Student" - Primer Level

F.D.L.312

How To Prepare Your Piano Lessons

1. Clap and sing the words.

2. Clap and count aloud.

3. See that your fingers are curved.

4. Use the correct fingering.

5. Count ALOUD as you play SLOWLY.

6. PLAY and SING.

When your lesson is prepared using the SIX STEPS above, place a check in the box below each piece.

You are now ready for your LESSON PRACTICE BOOK, David Carr Glover Piano Library.

TEACHER: Flash Cards are available for this Level.

F.D.L.312

The Keyboard

The keyboard has black and white keys.

The black keys are divided into groups of twos and threes.

With a pencil circle all groups of two black keys.

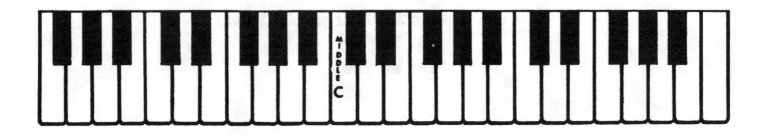

With a pencil circle all groups of three black keys.

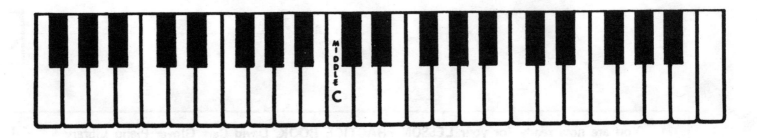

You are now ready for a new book PIANO THEORY, David Carr Glover Piano Library - Primer Level.

Tones From Your Keyboard

Beginning at the lowest part of your keyboard:

1. Locate and play together all two black groups.

2. Locate and play together all three black groups.

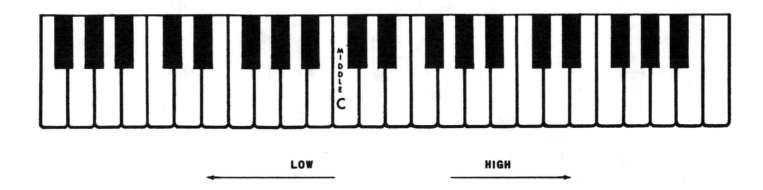

Did you hear the LOW and HIGH tones as you played?

LOW tones were <u>below</u> (to the left) Middle C.

HIGH tones were <u>above</u> (to the right) Middle C.

F.D.L.312

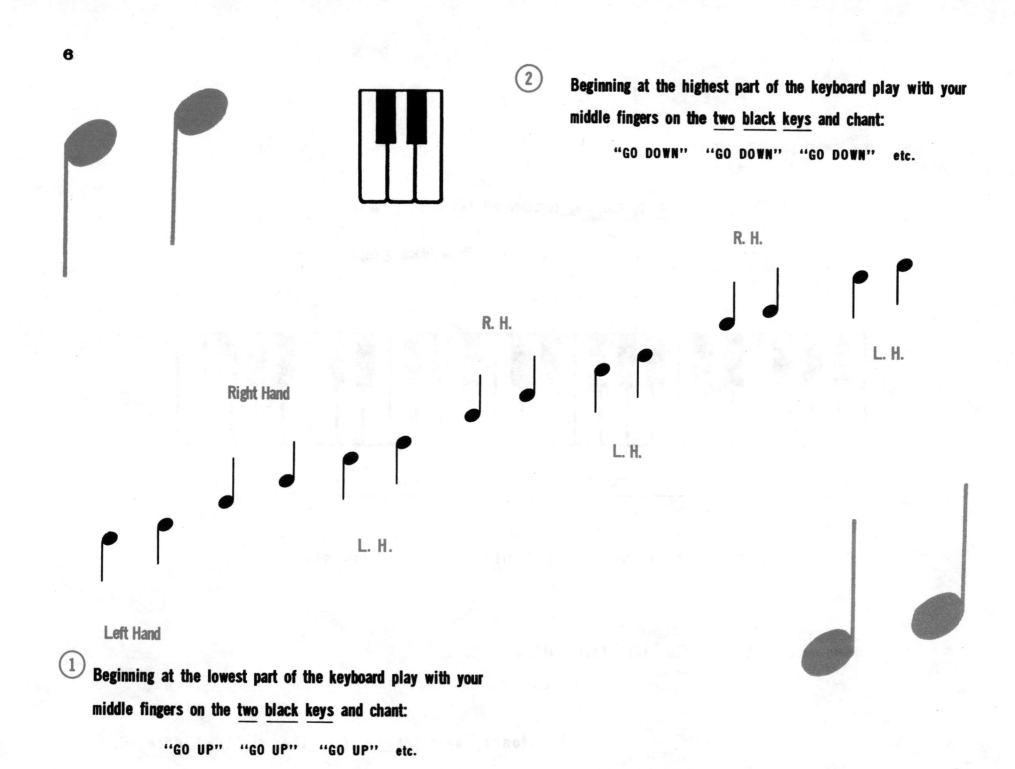

② Beginning at the highest part of the keyboard play with your middle fingers on the <u>two</u> <u>black</u> <u>keys</u> and chant:

"GO DOWN" "GO DOWN" "GO DOWN" etc.

R. H.

R. H.

Right Hand

L. H.

L. H.

L. H.

Left Hand

① Beginning at the lowest part of the keyboard play with your middle fingers on the <u>two</u> <u>black</u> <u>keys</u> and chant:

"GO UP" "GO UP" "GO UP" etc.

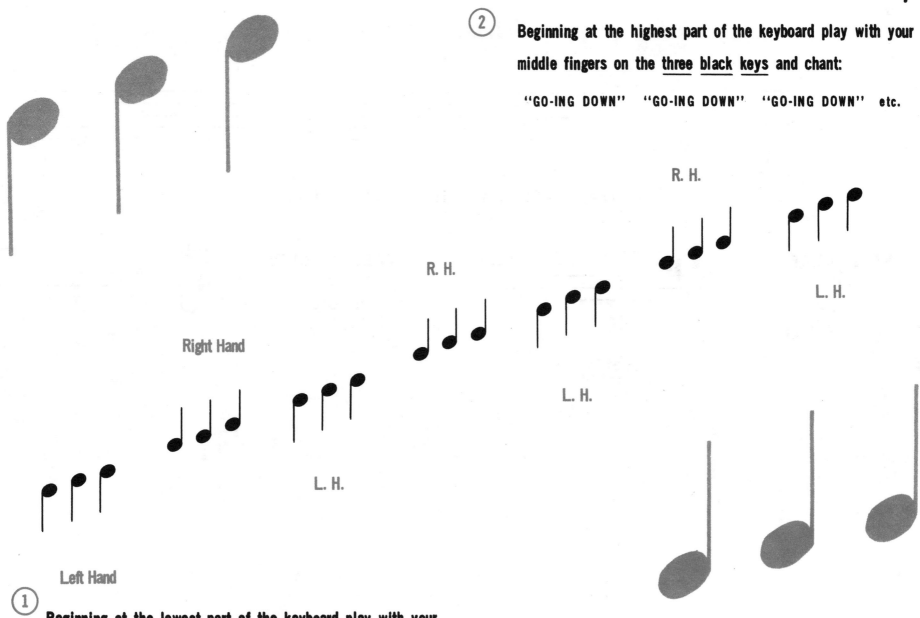

② Beginning at the highest part of the keyboard play with your middle fingers on the **three** **black** **keys** and chant:

"GO-ING DOWN"   "GO-ING DOWN"   "GO-ING DOWN"   etc.

R. H.

R. H.

L. H.

R. H.

L. H.

Right Hand

L. H.

Left Hand

① Beginning at the lowest part of the keyboard play with your middle fingers on the **three** **black** **keys** and chant:

"GO-ING UP"   "GO-ING UP"   "GO-ING UP"   etc.

We Begin To Read

STAFF

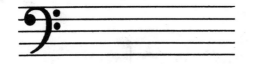

The STAFF has 5 lines and 4 spaces.

**BASS CLEF
or
F Clef**

**TREBLE CLEF
or
G Clef**

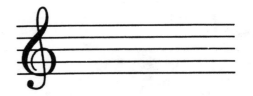

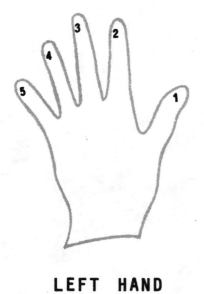

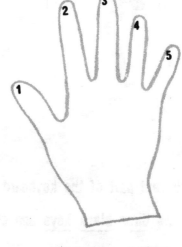

LEFT HAND

RIGHT HAND

F.D.L.312

GRAND STAFF

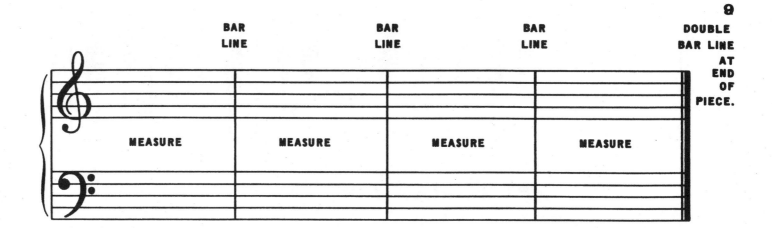

BAR LINE   BAR LINE   BAR LINE   DOUBLE BAR LINE AT END OF PIECE.

MEASURE   MEASURE   MEASURE   MEASURE

KEYBOARD

MUSICAL ALPHABET

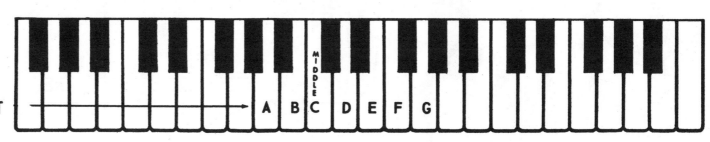

A B C D E F G

Notes are placed on the Grand Staff and tell us what keys to play.

Notes may be placed with lines through them ━⊖━ or in spaces ⟁

Notes move up. — Notes move down. — Notes are repeated.

Teacher: The David Carr Glover Music Magic Slate is available for this level.

F.D.L.312

Right Hand — Locate and play all C's and D's together - beginning with Middle C and D.

Left Hand — Locate and play all C's and B's together - beginning with Middle C and B.

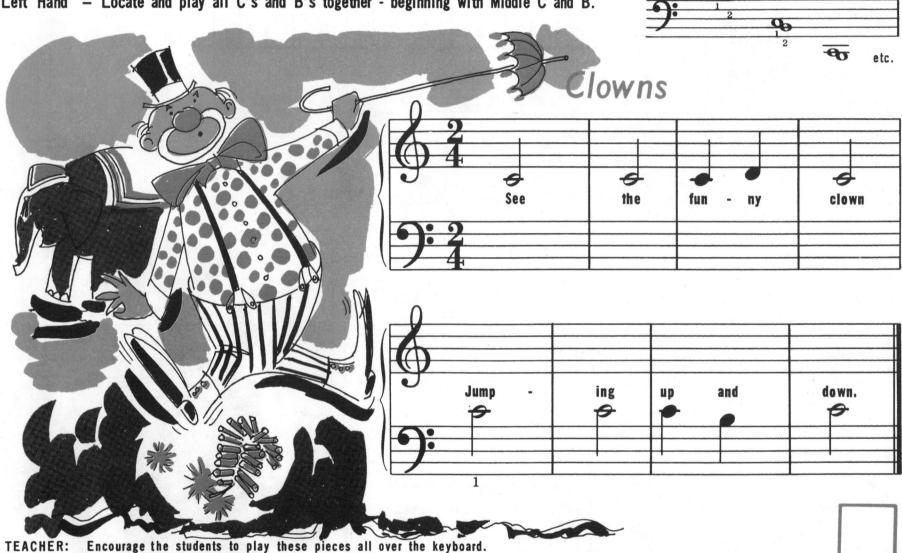

Clowns

See the fun - ny clown

Jump - ing up and down.

TEACHER: Encourage the students to play these pieces all over the keyboard.

F.D.L.312

You are now ready for a new book 30 NOTE SPELLING LESSONS, David Carr Glover Piano Library - Primer Level.

Dotted Half Note

$\daleth \cdot$ = 3 Beats

Locate and play all E's.

Time or Meter Signature

3 → Beats to each measure

4 → Each Quarter Note receives 1 Beat

Little White Pony

Lit - tle white   po - ny is   danc -   ing,

Lit - tle   white   po - ny is   pranc -   ing.

14

Locate and play all A's.

A B MIDDLE C

3 2 1

One Rainy Day

Go a-way Go a-way Rain - drops,

1 2 3   3

Come a - gain Come a - gain Sun - shine.

ONE RAINY DAY

Second Part

rit.

F.D.L.312

Right Hand — Locate and play all C's, D's, and E's together - beginning with Middle C, D and E.

Left Hand — Locate and play all C's, B's, and A's together - beginning with Middle C, B and A.

etc.

Lullaby

Hush! my child - ren, Ba - by's sleep - ing.

LULLABY
Second Part

Whole Note

○ = 4 Beats

Time or Meter Signature

4 ——→ Beats to each measure

4 ——→ Each Quarter Note receives 1 Beat

Indian Boy

Once there was an In - dian boy and he would play

Indian Boy

On his tom - tom, On his tom - tom Night and day.

Indian Boy

Second Part

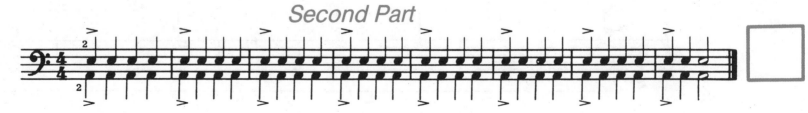

Hot Cross Buns

Quarter Rest

𝄽 = 1 Beat

TEACHER –

EGG FOO YONG and HOT CROSS BUNS

played together – – – – lots of fun.

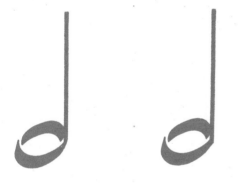

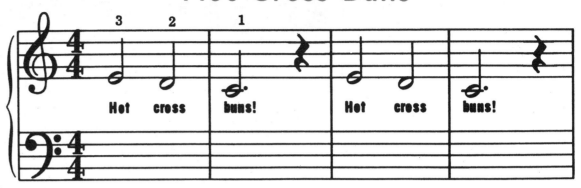

Hot   cross   buns!   Hot   cross   buns!

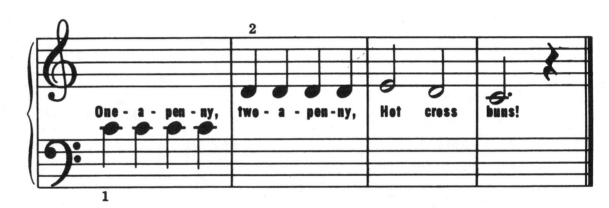

One - a - pen - ny,   two - a - pen - ny,   Hot   cross   buns!

Egg Foo Yong

Egg   foo   yong!   Egg   foo   yong!

One - a - pen - ny,   two - a - pen - ny,   Egg   foo   yong!

TEACHER: The Quarter Rest is presented at this point to help the student FEEL the musical phrase.

A Trip to Mars

A curved line, SLUR, over or under a group of notes is called a phrase mark.

A PHRASE is a musical thought played in a smooth and connected way – LEGATO. Lift the wrist gently at the end of the phrase making a small break in the sound without interrupting the rhythm.

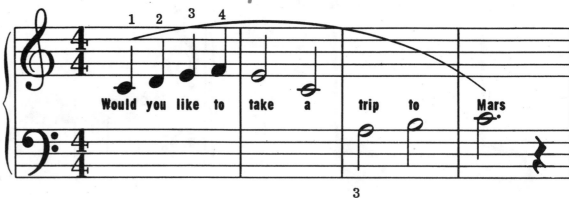

Would you like to take a trip to Mars

Way up in the sky a - mong the stars?

You are now ready for a new book PIANO REPERTOIRE (Folk Songs - Original Solos), David Carr Glover Piano Library - Primer Level.

F.D.L. 312

f is the abbreviation for FORTE which means loud.

p is the abbreviation for PIANO which means soft.

March

f Left, Right, Left, Right, Sol - diers are so near

p Left, Right, Left, Right, Sol - diers dis - ap - pear.

MARCH
Second Part

C Right Hand

f F Left Hand *p*

F.D.L. 312

My Kite

f Like an eag-le on the wing it flies so high

p See my kite go sail-ing in the blue, blue sky.

The CHURCH MUSICIAN - Primer Level from the David Carr Glover Sacred Music Piano Library is recommended at this time. This is a repertoire book of traditional and new religious music.

This is a TIE.

The second note is Tied to the first note. Play the first note only and let it sound for the value of both notes.

Echo

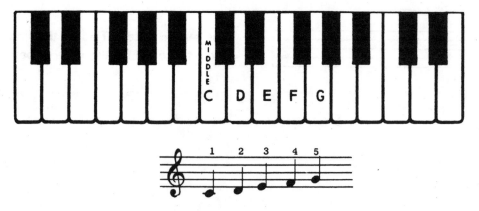

Sur le Pont d'Avignon

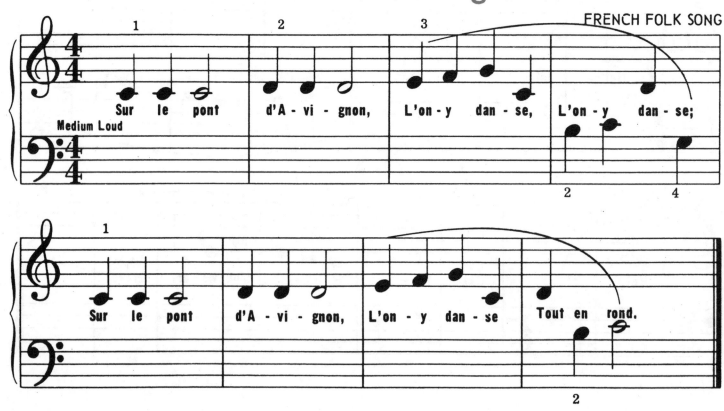

FRENCH FOLK SONG

Medium Loud

Sur le pont d'A - vi - gnon, L'on-y dan - se, L'on-y dan - se;

Sur le pont d'A - vi - gnon, L'on - y dan - se Tout en rond.

You are now ready for four new solos CAPTAIN CANDY, HENRY THE CAT, FUNNY BUNNY, and BABY CIRCUS ELEPHANT.

Camptown Races

STEPHEN FOSTER

f Camp-town la - dies sing this song Doo - dah! Doo - dah!

Camp-town race-track five miles long O! Doo - dah Day.

CAMPTOWN RACES
Second Part

mf

F.D.L.312

You are now ready for David Carr Glover's My Music World, Primer Level, Number One.

RIT. is the abbreviation for RITARDANDO.	It means to play gradually slower.

Morning Song

GRIEG

WHOLE MEASURE REST IN $\frac{4}{4}$ METER   ▬▬ = 4 BEATS

Resting

MORNING SONG *pp*

Second Part

A Big Bull Frog

f Eve-ry night a | big bull frog sits | on a lil - y | pad.

"Creak! Croak! Creak! Croak!" | He does sing a | song so strange and | sad.

A dot above ● or below ● a note means to play detached — not connected.
This is called STACCATO.

Little Chug Boat

Play
Hands
Together

LITTLE CHUG BOAT

Second Part

Tick, Tock, Clock

| WHOLE MEASURE REST IN $\frac{3}{4}$ METER | ▬ = | 3 Beats |

Good-bye, Summer

This is a SHARP ♯   When it is placed before a note PLAY THE NEXT KEY TO THE RIGHT.

SHARPS GO UP!

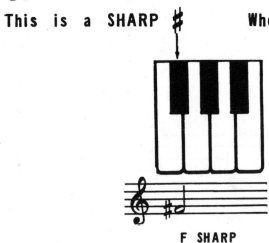

F SHARP

For chimes effect, press this Pedal down throughout the piece using the Right Foot.

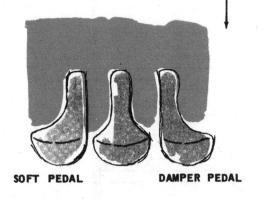

SOFT PEDAL   DAMPER PEDAL

THEN, VERY SOFTLY REPEAT ONE OCTAVE HIGHER – WITHOUT LIFTING PEDAL.

Chimes

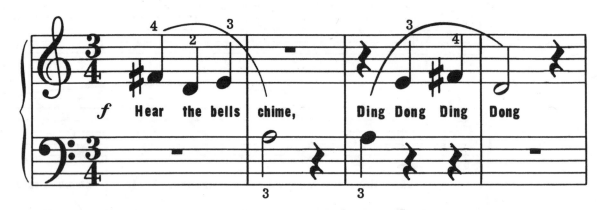

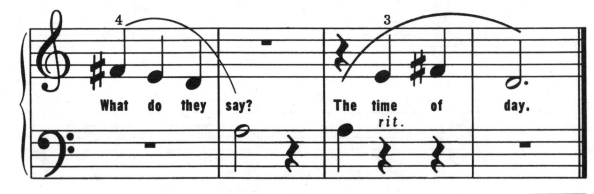

Dutch Dance

f Clip, Clop, Clop, Clip, Clop, Clop, All in a twirl,

Hap-py Dutch boy and a hap-py Dutch girl.

F# at the beginning of a piece means that all F's are to be played sharp.
This is called G MAJOR KEY SIGNATURE.

Half Rest

= 2 Beats

Steam Shovel

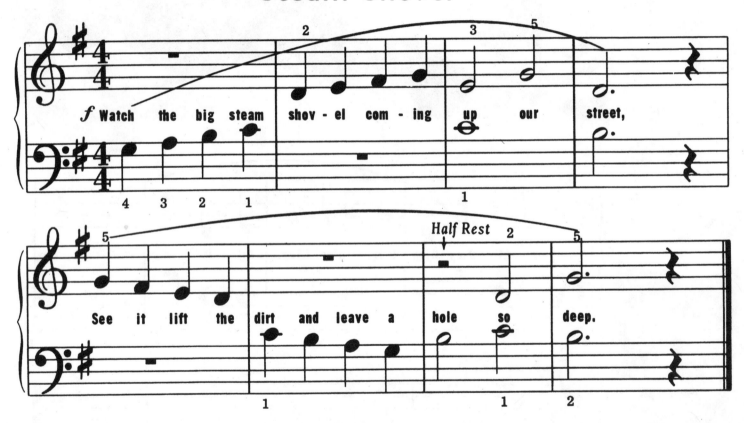

You are now ready for three new solos CALICO WALTZ, BATTER UP, and PICNIC IN THE PARK.

F.D.L. 312

Mister Wiggle Nose

Key Signature

p Mis - ter Rab - bit Wig - gle nose, nib - ble nib - ble fast,

f Watch out for the dan - de - lion Hid - ing in the grass.

Add Meter Signatures to the Following Music

F.D.L.312

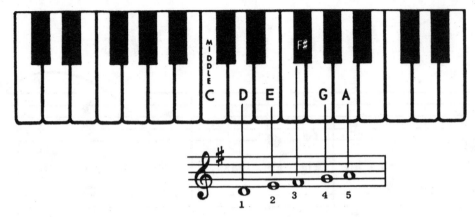

Good King Wenceslas

New Hand Position

f Good King Wen-ces - las looked out, On the Feast of Ste - phen,

Where the snow lay round a - bout, Deep and crisp and e - ven.

GOOD KING WENCESLAS
Second Part

r.h.

l.h. *f*

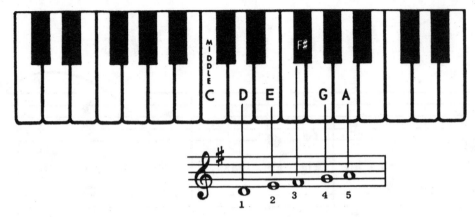

Good King Wenceslas

34

F.D.L.312

Snowflakes

How many beats do the following notes receive in $\frac{4}{4}$ METER?

Snow - flakes flut - ter in the air so light,

Soon the roof tops will be spark - ling white.

F.D.L.312

This is a FLAT ♭   When it is placed before a note, PLAY THE NEXT KEY TO THE LEFT.

FLATS GO DOWN!

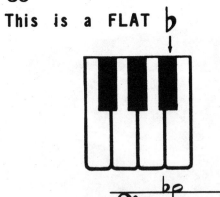

This Old Man

NOTE: When played as a duet, play *THIS OLD MAN* one octave higher.

THIS OLD MAN

Second Part

Bb at the beginning of a piece means that all B's are to be played flat.

This is called the F MAJOR KEY SIGNATURE.

Big Fat Frog

f Once there was a big, fat frog Made his home in-side a log;

Hop, Hop, Hop, Hop, Hop, Hop, Mis - ter big, fat frog.

Left Hand Finger Fun

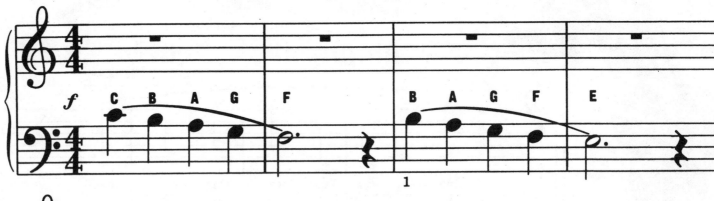

Play Finger Fun three ways:

Loud,

   Soft,

      and

   Staccato.

You are now ready for four new solos HERE COMES THE BAND, CHASE ME, "HANTS", and THE MONKEY AND THE KANGAROO.

Bass Clef Note Spelling

Write the letter names under these notes.
(They spell words.)

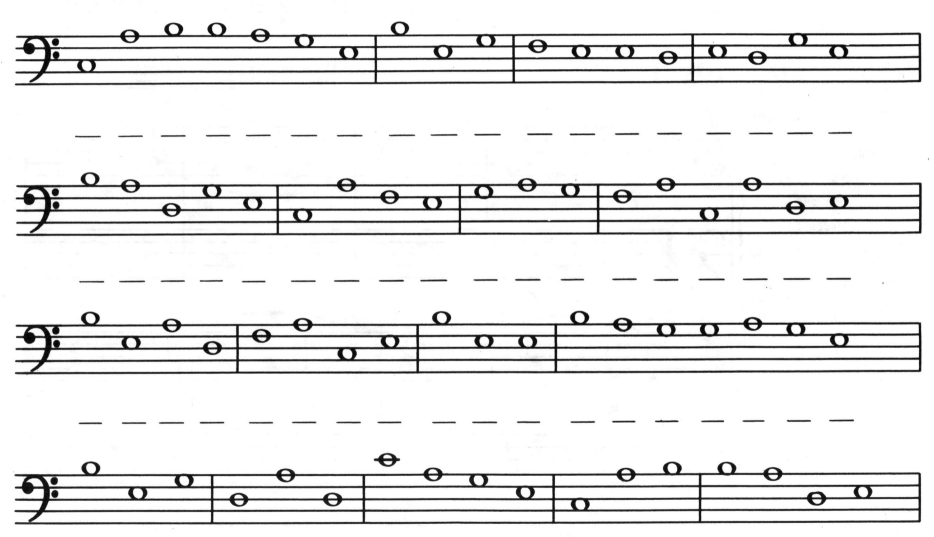

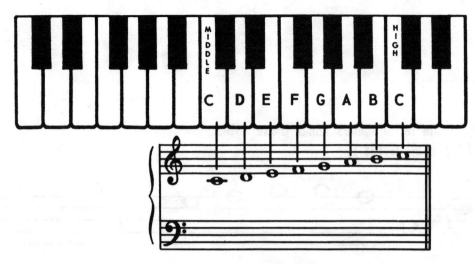

Right Hand Finger Fun

Play Finger Fun three ways:

Loud,

Soft,

and

Staccato.

You are now ready for David Carr Glover's My Music World, Primer Level Number Two.

Treble Clef Note Spelling

Write the letter names under these notes.
(They spell words.)

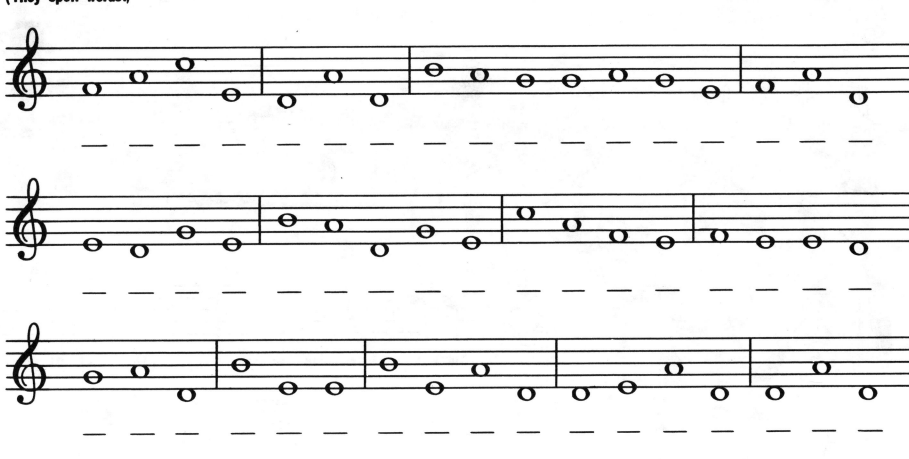

Old Mac Donald

FOLK SONG

Note: When played as a duet, play OLD MacDONALD one octave higher.

OLD MAC DONALD

Second Part

You are now ready for three new solos SUGAR COOKIES, YO HO! THE SAILOR'S SONG, and CALLIOPE.

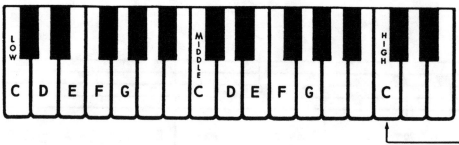

This note is to be played by the 2nd finger, Left Hand.

Three Mice on a Harp

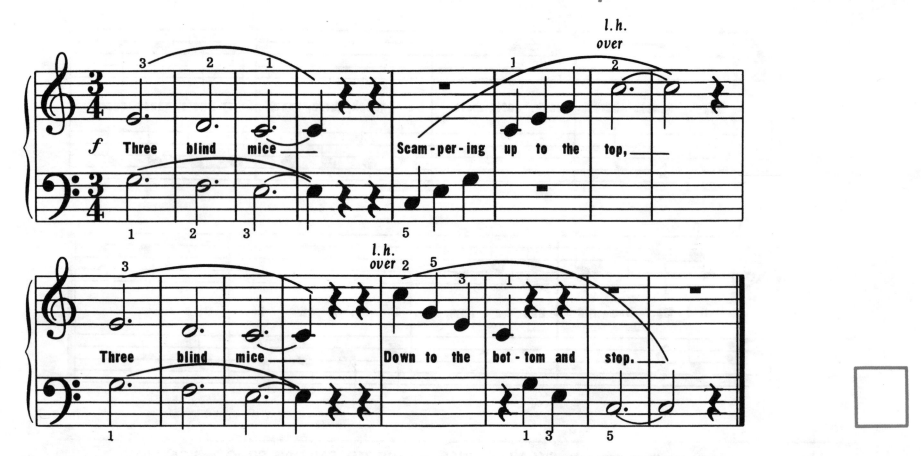

Certificate of Award

THIS IS TO CERTIFY THAT _____

HAS COMPLETED

PIANO STUDENT

PRIMER LEVEL

OF THE

David Carr Glover
PIANO LIBRARY

_____   _____
Date   Teacher